For _____

From _____

Be nice to yourself!

Lives ... Get One

Illustrated by
Mary Engelbreit

**Andrews McMeel
Publishing**

Kansas City

Lives . . . Get One copyright © 1997 by Mary Engelbreit Ink. All rights reserved. Printed in Singapore. No part of this book may be used or reproduced in any manner whatsoever without written permission except in the case of reprints in the context of reviews. For information write Andrews McMeel Publishing, an Andrews McMeel Universal company, 4520 Main Street, Kansas City, Missouri 64111.

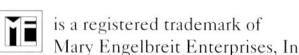 is a registered trademark of Mary Engelbreit Enterprises, Inc.

www.andrewsmcmeel.com

ISBN: 0-8362-2778-6

Written by Jan Miller Girando

Lives...Get One

The hustle-bustle hurry
that we live in
can keep us jumping,
always on the run.
It's one thing or another
every minute.
We've got to get a life
and have some fun!

We zoom about,
performing as expected.
Time flies as we
accomplish every task.

If there's a job to do,
we're always willing.
If someone needs a favor,
they just ask.

"Make everybody happy"
is our credo...
be conscientious,
never count the cost.

Become the person
everyone relies on...
the one without whose help
all would be lost.

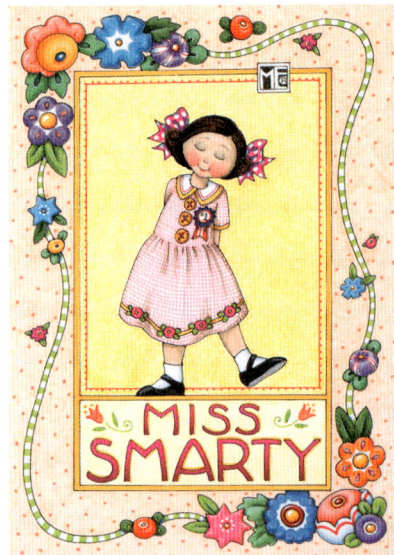

Our days are check-marks
on a long "To Do" list...
priorities seem
out of whack somehow.

It's time
to make some changes
and start living!
We've got to get a life,
beginning now!

Remember things
that used to be relaxing?
The wake-up call
of robins in the spring?

A magic moment
basking in the sunset?
The wonder gazing
at the stars can bring?

Recall the things
that used to give us pleasure
before we started
putting others first...

A furry friend
that helped to boost our spirits
whenever we were feeling
at our worst...

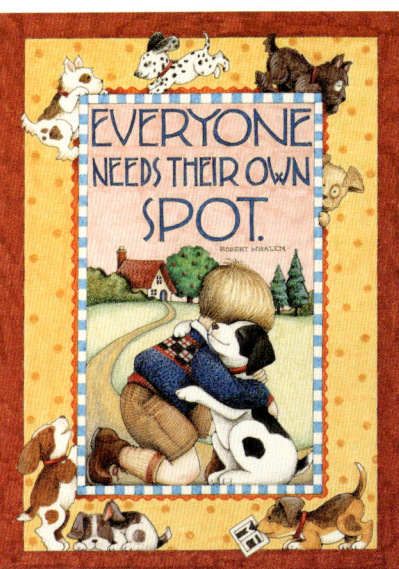

The promise of a brilliant morning sunrise...

A chatty letter from a favorite friend...

A painted rainbow
from a passing cloudburst...
a confidant on whom
we can depend.

It's time we took control
of how we're living
by doing more
of everything we like.

Create a watercolor!
Learn piano!
Begin a course in Bonsai!
Ride a bike!

We need to nourish
talents we've neglected...
who knows what
revelations lie ahead...

And if we're not quite ready
to get active,
allow ourselves to spend
all day in bed!

Perhaps the wanderlust commands our spirit! Who cares if friends and loved ones are surprised?

We've earned the right
to be a bit indulgent,
and that's the way we get
re-energized!

It's great to be responsible,
but face it—
we all need some relief
from daily stress.

It's up to us to make
each day rewarding
and give ourselves
the gift of happiness.